Torque brims with excitement perfect for thrill-seekers of all kinds. Discover daring survival skills, explore uncharted worlds, and marvel at mighty engines and extreme sports. In *Torque* books, anything can happen. Are you ready?

This edition first published in 2026 by Bellwether Media, Inc.

No part of this publication may be reproduced in whole or in part without written **permission** of the publisher. For information regarding permission, write to Bellwether Media, Inc., Attention: Permissions **Department**, 3500 American Blvd W, Suite 150, Bloomington, MN 55431.

Library of Congress Cataloging-in-Publication Data

Names: Birdoff, Ariel Factor, author.
Title: Luke Combs / Ariel Factor Birdoff.
Description: Minneapolis, MN : Bellwether Media, 2026. | Series: Music superstars | Includes bibliographical references and index. | Audience: Ages 7-12 | Audience: Grades 4-6 | Summary: "Engaging images accompany information about Luke Combs. The combination of high-interest subject matter and light text is intended for students in grades 3 through 7"– Provided by publisher.
Identifiers: LCCN 2025001558 (print) | LCCN 2025001559 (ebook) | ISBN 9798893045024 (library binding) | ISBN 9798893046403 (ebook)
Subjects: LCSH: Combs, Luke–Juvenile literature. | Singers–Uited States–Biography–Juvenile literature. | Country musicians–Uited States–Biography–Juvenile literature. | LCGFT: Biographies.
Classification: LCC ML3930.C537 B57 2026 (print) | LCC ML3930.C537 (ebook) | DDC 782.421642092 [B]–dc23/eng/20250117
LC record available at https://lccn.loc.gov/2025001558
LC ebook record available at https://lccn.loc.gov/2025001559

Text copyright © 2026 by Bellwether Media, Inc. TORQUE and associated logos are trademarks and/or registered trademarks of Bellwether Media, Inc. Bellwether Media is a division of FlutterBee Education Group.

Editor: Rachael Barnes   Designer: Josh Brink

Printed in the United States of America, North Mankato, MN.

TABLE OF CONTENTS

A Storm on Stage!	4
Who Is Luke Combs?	6
Practice, Practice, Practice!	8
What You See Is What You Get	12
Bootleggers and Beyond	20
Glossary	22
To Learn More	23
Index	24

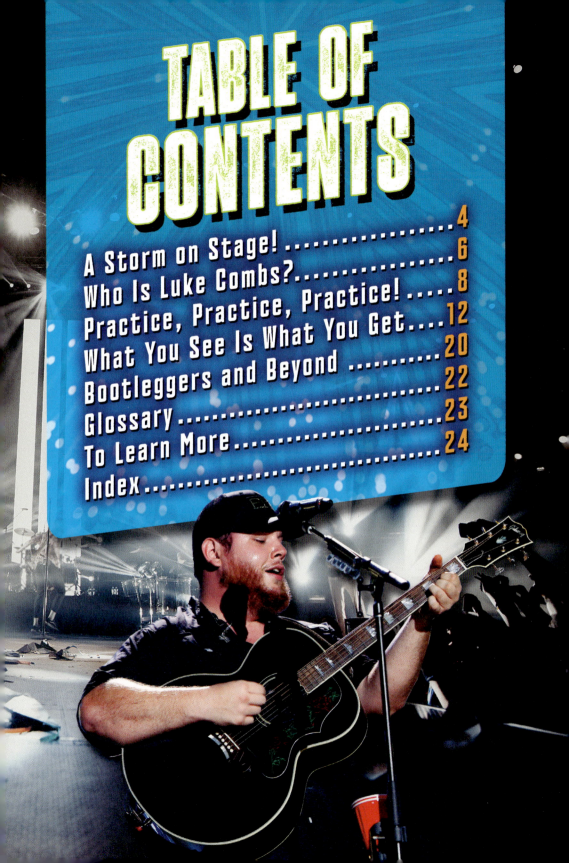

A STORM ON STAGE!

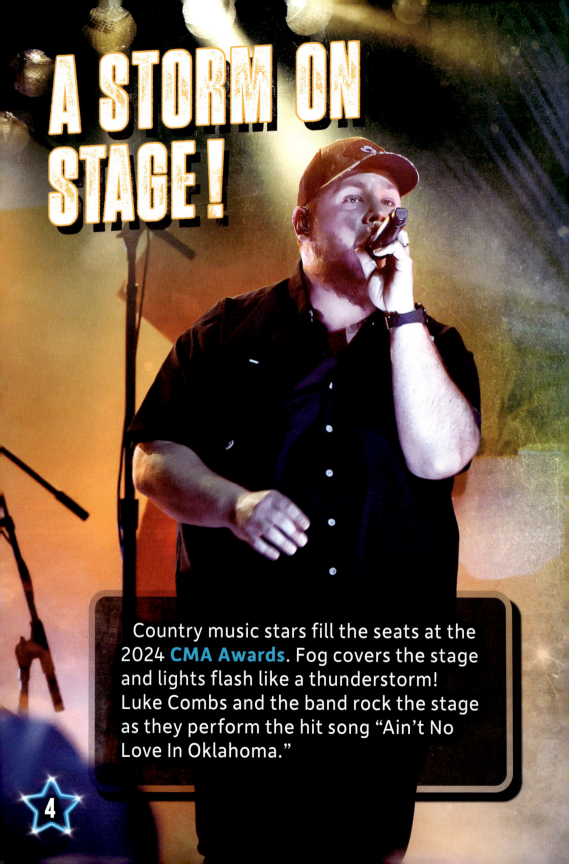

Country music stars fill the seats at the 2024 **CMA Awards**. Fog covers the stage and lights flash like a thunderstorm! Luke Combs and the band rock the stage as they perform the hit song "Ain't No Love In Oklahoma."

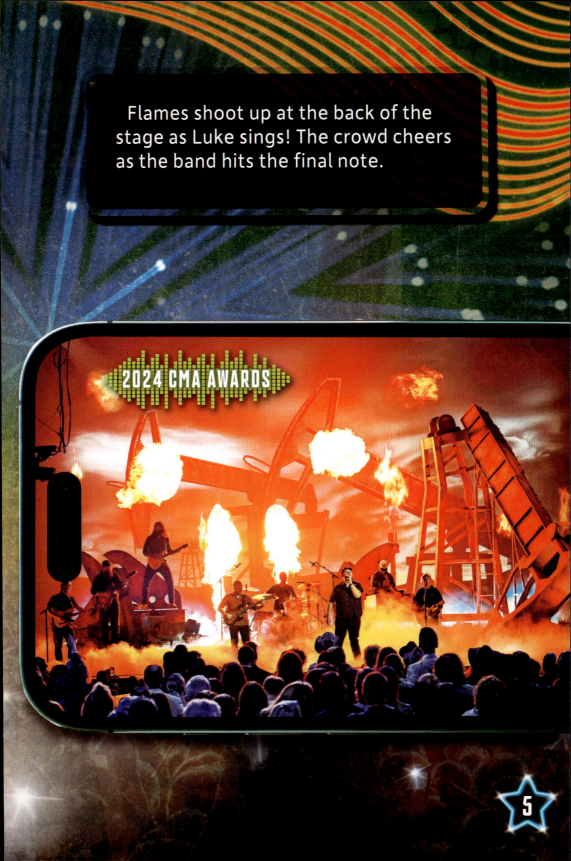

Flames shoot up at the back of the stage as Luke sings! The crowd cheers as the band hits the final note.

WHO IS LUKE COMBS?

Luke Combs is a country music artist. He has been writing and singing for more than 10 years. He is known for his style and **authentic** music. He performs to huge crowds around the world!

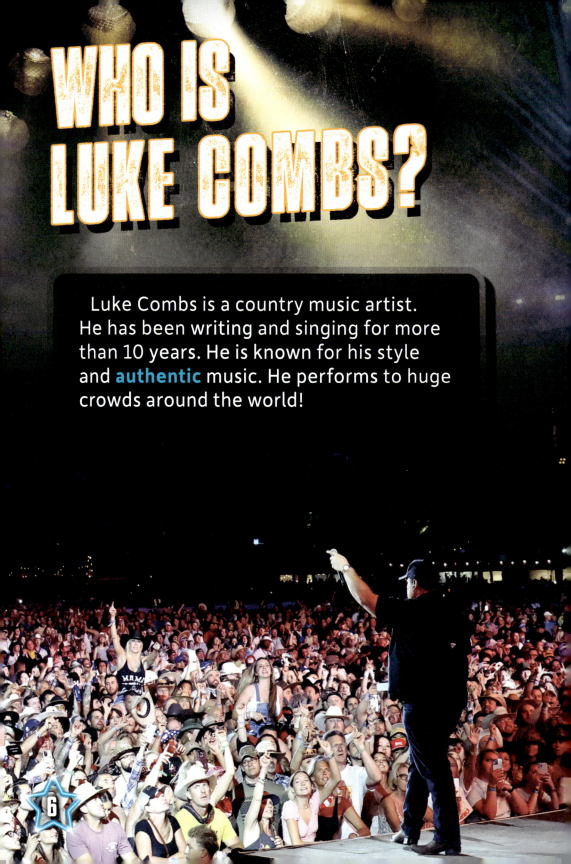

LUKE COMBS

Birthday
March 2, 1990

Hometown
Asheville, North Carolina

Type of Music
country

First Solo Hit
"Hurricane"

Luke is open about his **mental health**. He shares his struggles and what has helped him. He hopes more people can get the help they need.

PRACTICE, PRACTICE, PRACTICE!

Luke was born on March 2, 1990. He grew up with his parents in Asheville, North Carolina.

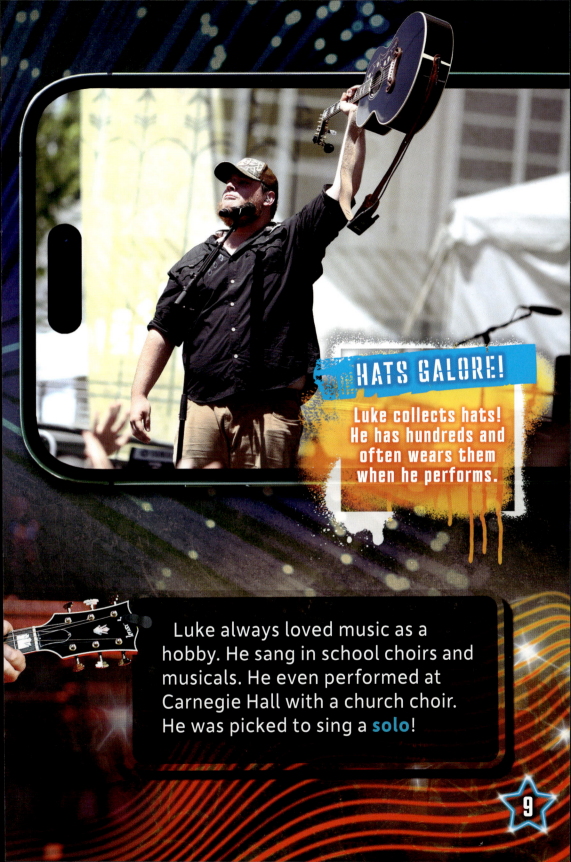

HATS GALORE!

Luke collects hats! He has hundreds and often wears them when he performs.

Luke always loved music as a hobby. He sang in school choirs and musicals. He even performed at Carnegie Hall with a church choir. He was picked to sing a **solo**!

When Luke was 21 years old, he taught himself how to play the guitar. He began writing songs and performing in North Carolina. People loved hearing him sing.

LUKE PERFORMING IN NORTH CAROLINA

FAVORITES

Color
blue

Scary Movie
It Follows

Cereal
Apple Jacks

Hobby
fishing

In 2014, Luke moved to Nashville, Tennessee. He **released** two **EPs** starting with *The Way She Rides*. Two years later, Luke signed with the Columbia Nashville **record label**.

11

WHAT YOU SEE IS WHAT YOU GET

Luke released his first full-length album in 2017. *This One's For You* reached number four on the *Billboard* 200 chart.

LUKE PERFORMING AT THE GRAND OLE OPRY

A COUNTRY MUSIC HONOR!

Luke was invited to be a member of the Grand Ole Opry in 2019. This honor is only offered to artists that have had a meaningful effect on country music.

The song "Hurricane" was a hit! It reached number one on the *Billboard* Hot Country Songs and the *Billboard* Country Airplay charts. "Hurricane" made Luke famous!

13

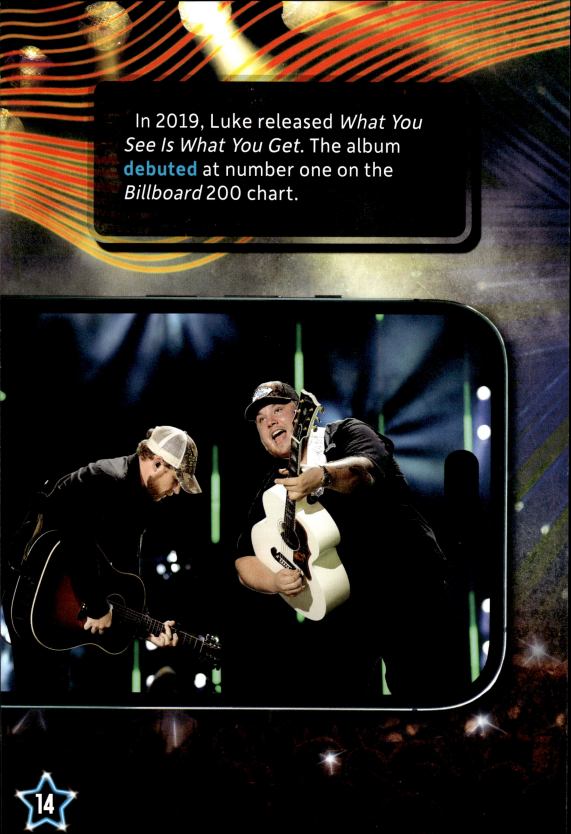

In 2019, Luke released *What You See Is What You Get*. The album **debuted** at number one on the *Billboard* 200 chart.

AWARDS
as of February 2025

5 ACM Awards

6 *Billboard* Music Awards

9 CMA Awards

7 iHeartRadio Music Awards

2020 CMA AWARDS

It went on to win Album of the Year at the 2020 CMA Awards. Luke was also named one of 2020's best country singers!

Luke's third album, *Growin' Up*, came out in 2022. It featured a **collaboration** with fellow country artist Miranda Lambert. Their song, "Outrunnin' Your Memory," was **nominated** for a **Grammy Award** in 2023.

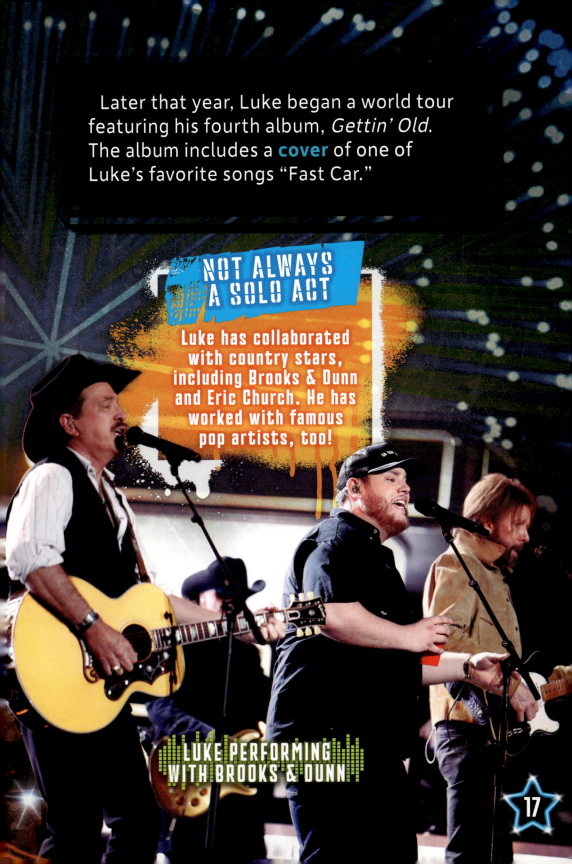

Later that year, Luke began a world tour featuring his fourth album, *Gettin' Old*. The album includes a **cover** of one of Luke's favorite songs "Fast Car."

NOT ALWAYS A SOLO ACT

Luke has collaborated with country stars, including Brooks & Dunn and Eric Church. He has worked with famous pop artists, too!

LUKE PERFORMING WITH BROOKS & DUNN

In June 2024, Luke released his fifth album, *Fathers & Sons*. The 12-song album talks about what it means to be a good father. It honors his two sons and other men in his family. No matter what he is singing about, Luke's music tells a story.

TIMELINE

– 2017 –
Luke releases his first album, *This One's For You*

– 2019 –
Luke releases his second album, *What You See Is What You Get*

— 2022 —
Luke releases his third album, *Growin' Up*

— 2024 —
Luke starts the Growin' Up and Gettin' Old Tour after releasing his fourth album

— 2024 —
Luke releases his fifth album, *Fathers & Sons*

BOOTLEGGERS AND BEYOND

Luke's fans are called Bootleggers. Luke keeps fans in mind when planning his live shows. He tries to make every night special!

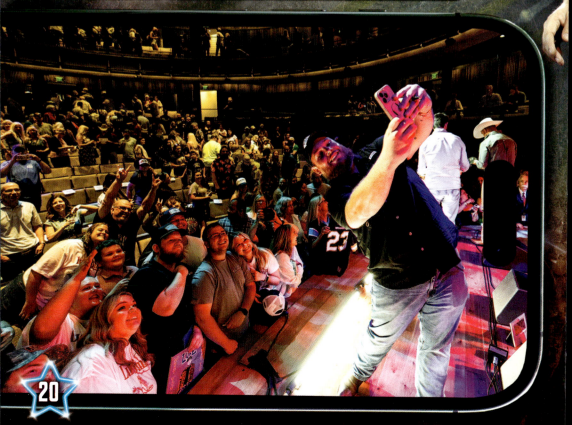

PLAYLIST

"Hurricane" (2015)

"When It Rains It Pours" (2017)

"Forever After All" (2019)

"Outrunnin' Your Memory" (2022)

"Love You Anyway" (2023)

Luke has given more than music to the world. In 2024, he helped raise $25 million to help people after a **natural disaster**. He continues to use music to help others. Fans cannot wait to see what Luke does next!

GLOSSARY

authentic—real

Billboard—related to a well-known music news magazine and website that ranks songs and albums

CMA Awards—a yearly event during which awards are presented for achievements in country music; CMA stands for Country Music Association.

collaboration—something created while working with others

cover—a new performance of a song by a different singer than the original artist

debuted—was introduced or released for the first time

EPs—music recordings that are shorter than an album but have more songs than a single; EP stands for extended play.

Grammy Award—an award given by the Recording Academy of the United States for an achievement in music; Grammy Awards are also called Grammys.

mental health—the way people think and feel about themselves and the world around them

natural disaster—a sudden event in nature that causes great damage or loss

nominated—chosen as a candidate for an award

record label—a company that sells music

released—made music available for listening

solo—a part in a piece of music performed by one person

TO LEARN MORE

AT THE LIBRARY

Becker, Trudy. *Country Music*. Mendota Heights, Minn.: Focus Readers, 2025.

Mahin, Michael. *Gizmos, Gadgets, and Guitars: The Story of Leo Fender*. New York, N.Y.: Henry Holt and Company, 2021.

Nguyen, Suzane. *Taylor Swift*. Minneapolis, Minn.: Bellwether Media, 2025.

ON THE WEB

FACTSURFER

Factsurfer.com gives you a safe, fun way to find more information.

1. Go to www.factsurfer.com.

2. Enter "Luke Combs" into the search box and click 🔍.

3. Select your book cover to see a list of related content.

INDEX

albums, 12, 14, 16, 17, 18
awards, 4–5, 15, 16
Billboard, 12, 13, 14
Bootleggers, 20
Brooks & Dunn, 17
childhood, 8, 9
Church, Eric, 17
Columbia Nashville, 11
EPs, 11
family, 8, 18
fans, 20, 21
favorites, 11
Grand Ole Opry, 13
hats, 9
instrument, 10
Lambert, Miranda, 16
mental health, 7
Nashville, Tennessee, 11
natural disaster, 21
North Carolina, 8, 10
playlist, 21
profile, 7
songs, 4, 10, 13, 16, 17, 18
timeline, 18–19
tour, 17
types of music, 6, 13, 15, 17

The images in this book are reproduced through the courtesy of: Jason Moore/ ZUMA Press Wire/ Alamy, front cover; Catsense, front cover (light effect); Taya Ovod, pp. 2-3; Debby Wong, p. 3; Theo Wargo/ Getty Images, pp. 4-5; Astrida Valigorsky/ WireImage/ Getty Images, pp. 5, 7; Amy Sussman/ Getty Images for Stagecoach/ Getty Images, pp. 6-7; Amy Harris/ AP Images, p. 7 (VIP pass); Jason Davis/ Getty Images, pp. 8-9; Sara Kauss/ Getty Images, p. 9; Jason Moore/ ZUMA Wire/ Alamy, p. 10; Tim Mosenfelder/ FilmMagic/ Getty Images, pp. 11, 12; Elena11, p. 11 (paint swatch); Filmgoer, p. 11 (*It Follows*); digitalreflections, p. 11 (Apple Jacks); Nikolay132, p. 11 (fishing lure); Kevin Mazur/ Getty Images, p. 13; Jason Kempin/ Getty Images, p. 14; Terry Wyatt/ Getty Images, p. 15; Amy Nichole Harris, p. 15 (ACM Awards); Kathy Hutchins, p. 15 (*Billboard* Music Award); s_bukley, p. 15 (CMA Awards); Tinseltown, p. 15 (iHeart Radio Music Award); John Shearer/ Getty Images, p. 16; Rich Fury/ ACMA2019/ Getty Images, p. 17; Amy E. Price/ Getty Images, pp. 18-19; BWM, pp. 18-19, 21; John Shearer/ Getty Images for the Country Music Hall of Fame and Museum/ Getty Images, p. 20; ChrisJamesRyanPhotography, p. 21; Ben Houdijk, p. 23.

24